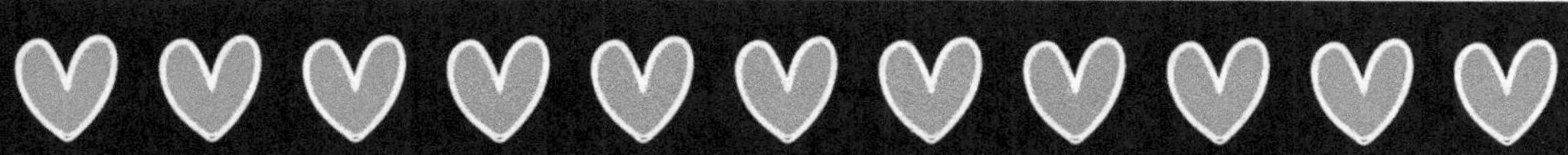

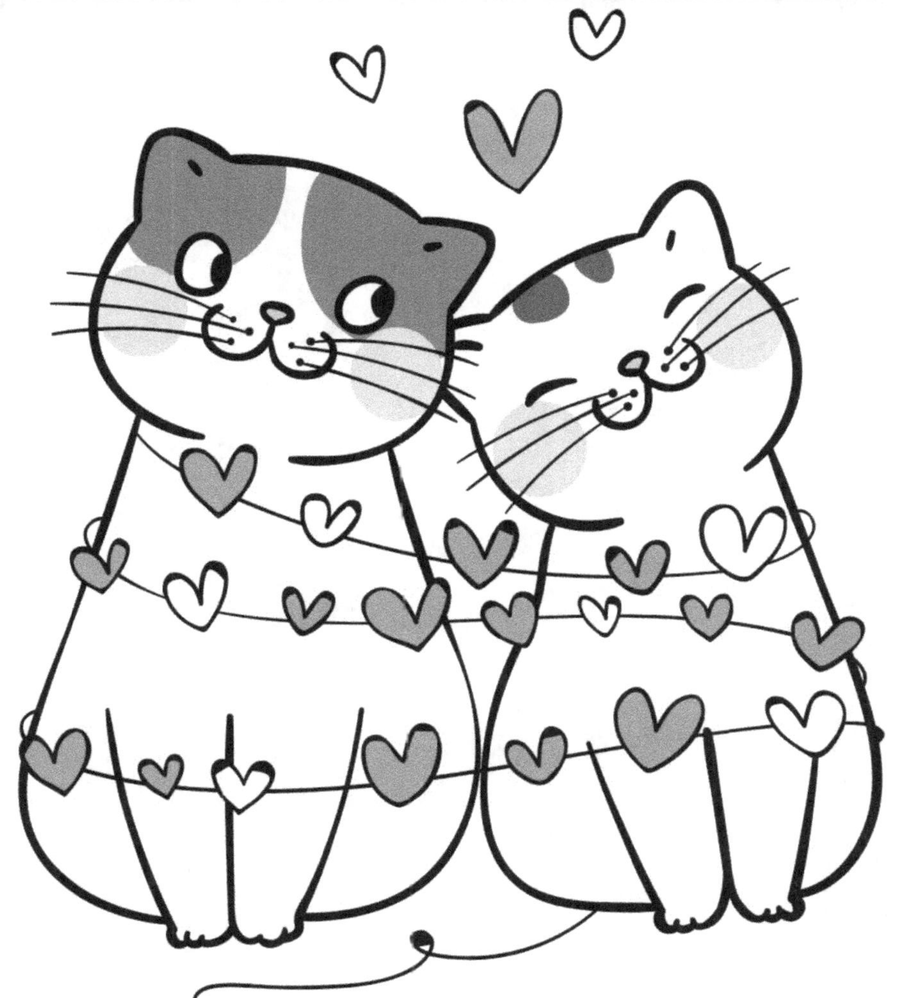

THIS BOOK BELONG TO ....

....

....

....

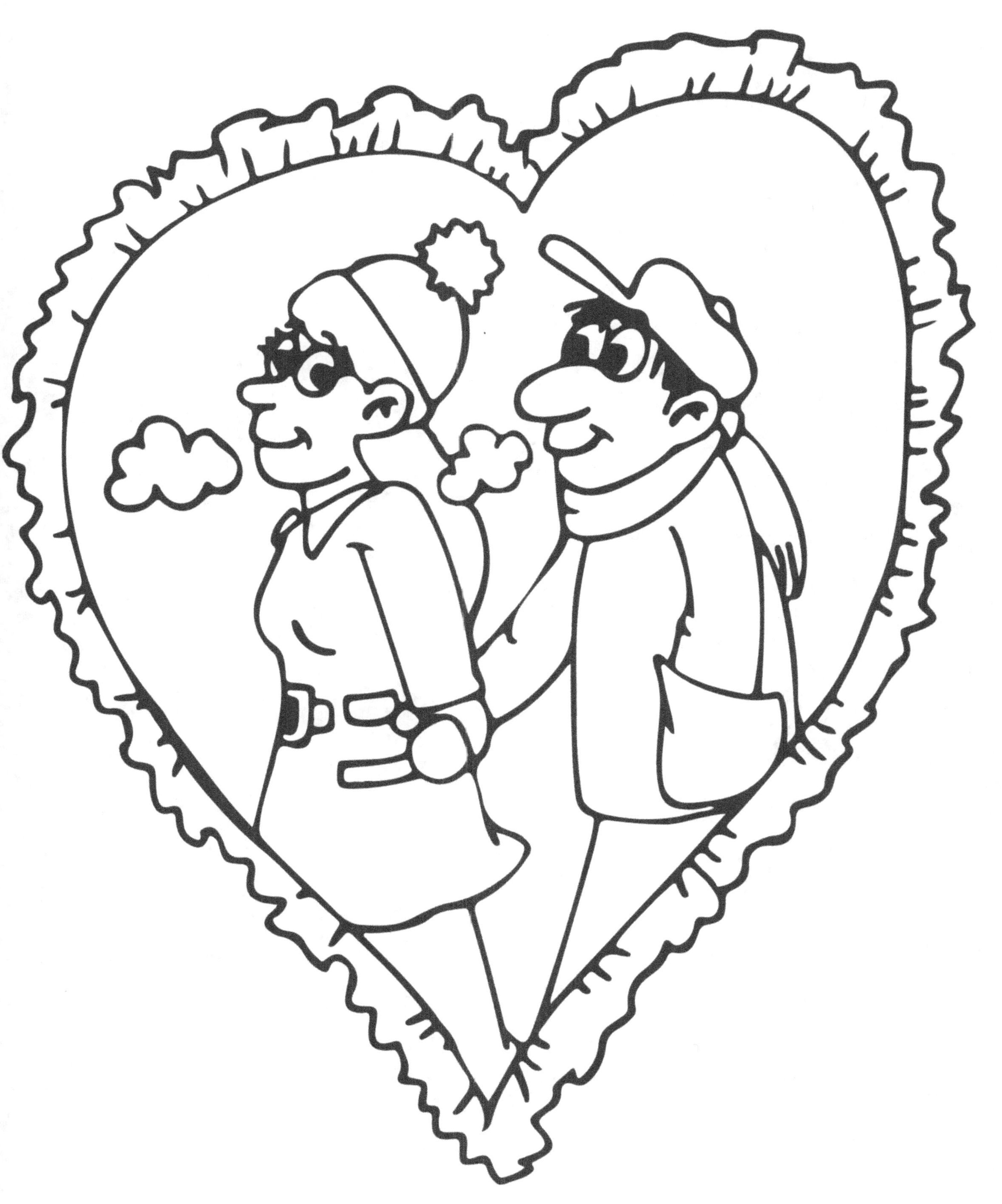

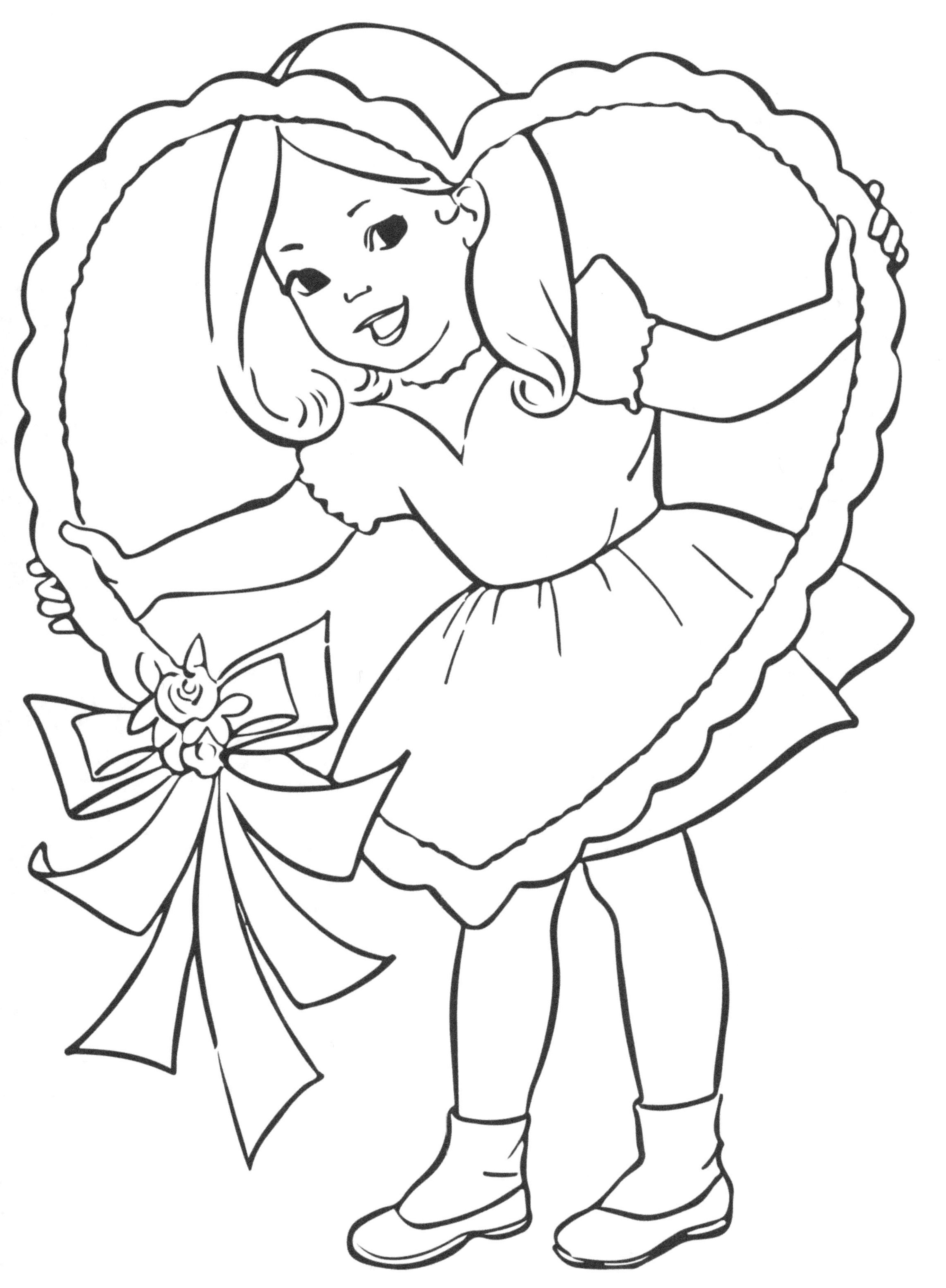

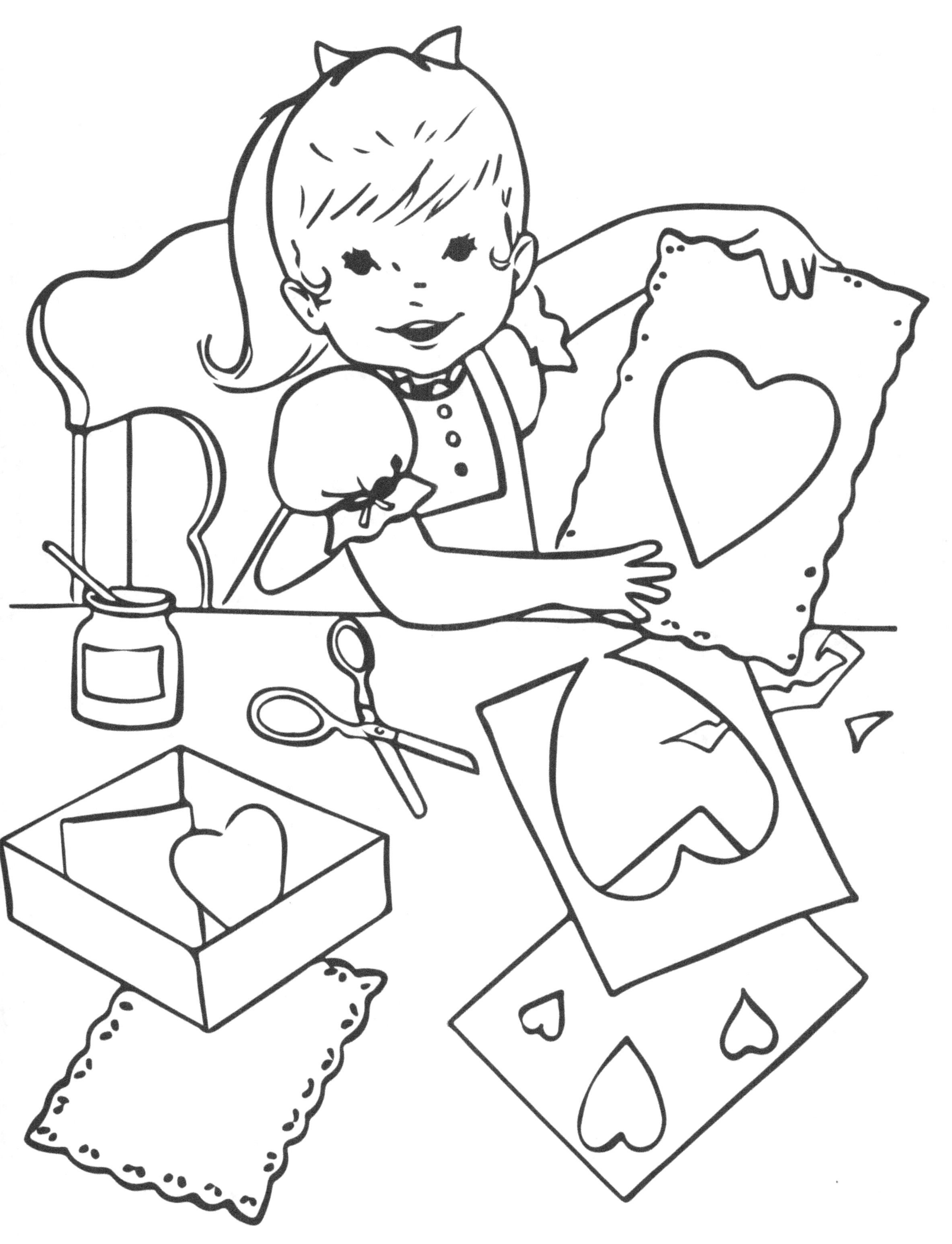

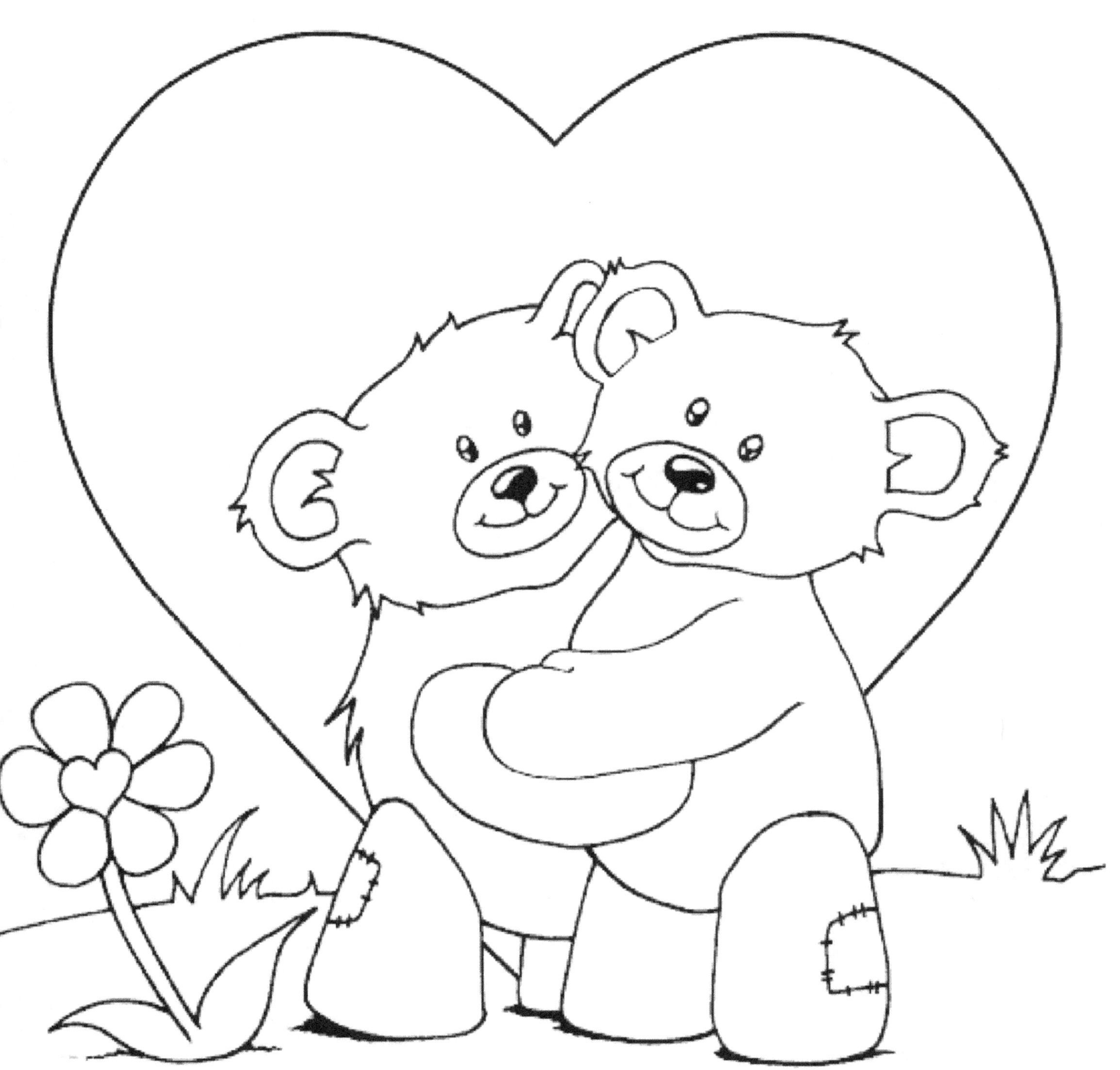

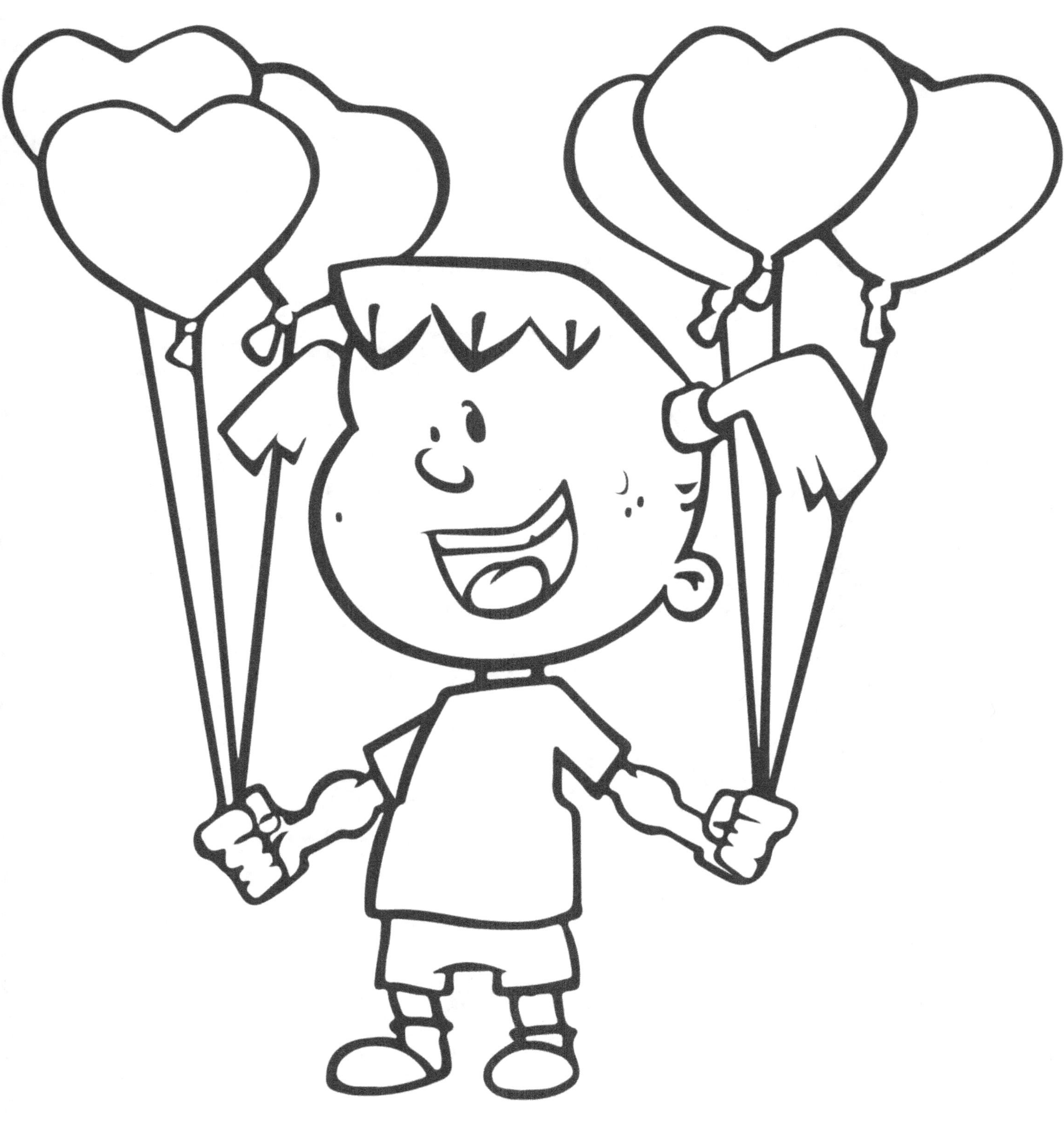

Happy
Valentine's Day

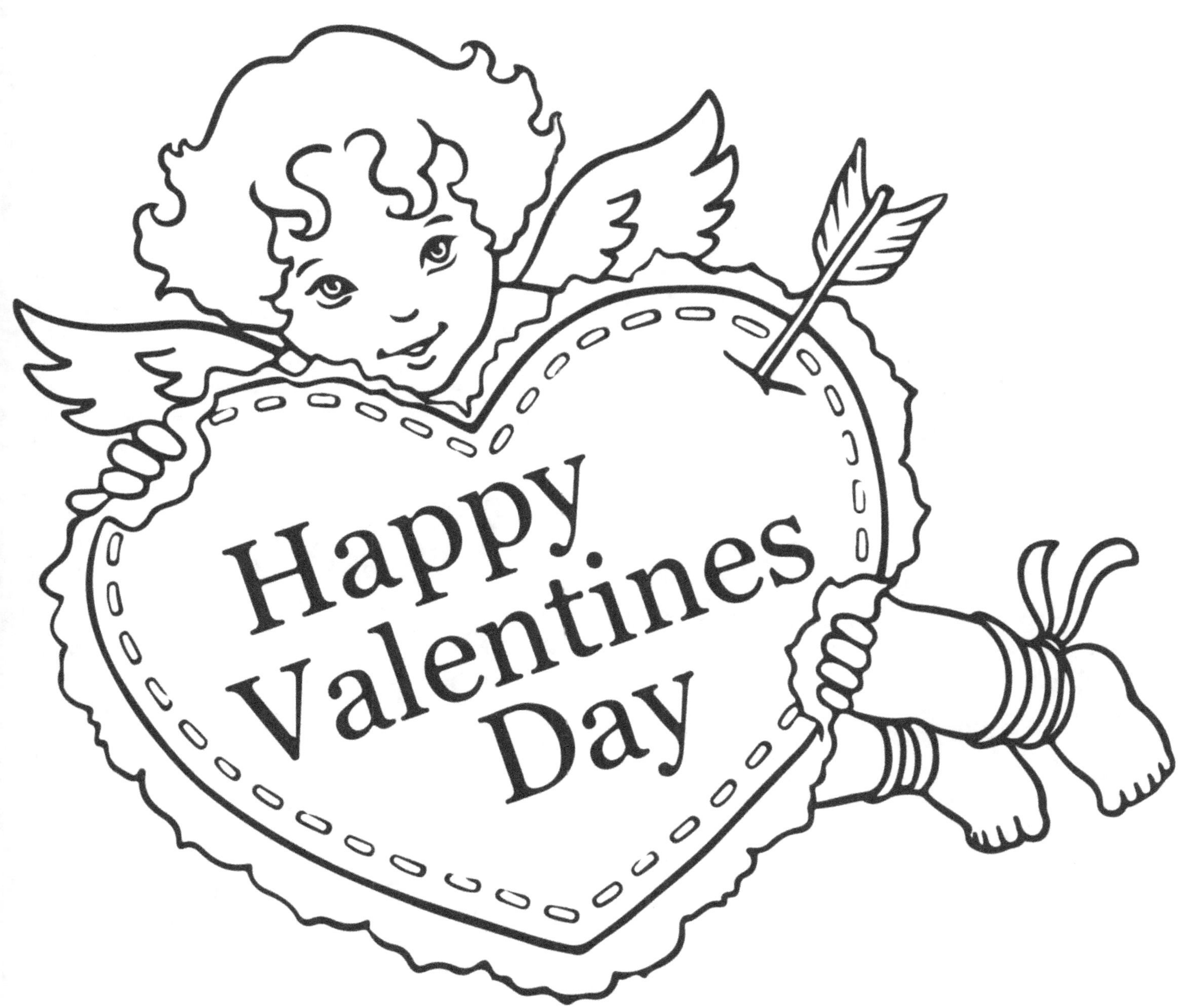

Happy
Valentines
Day

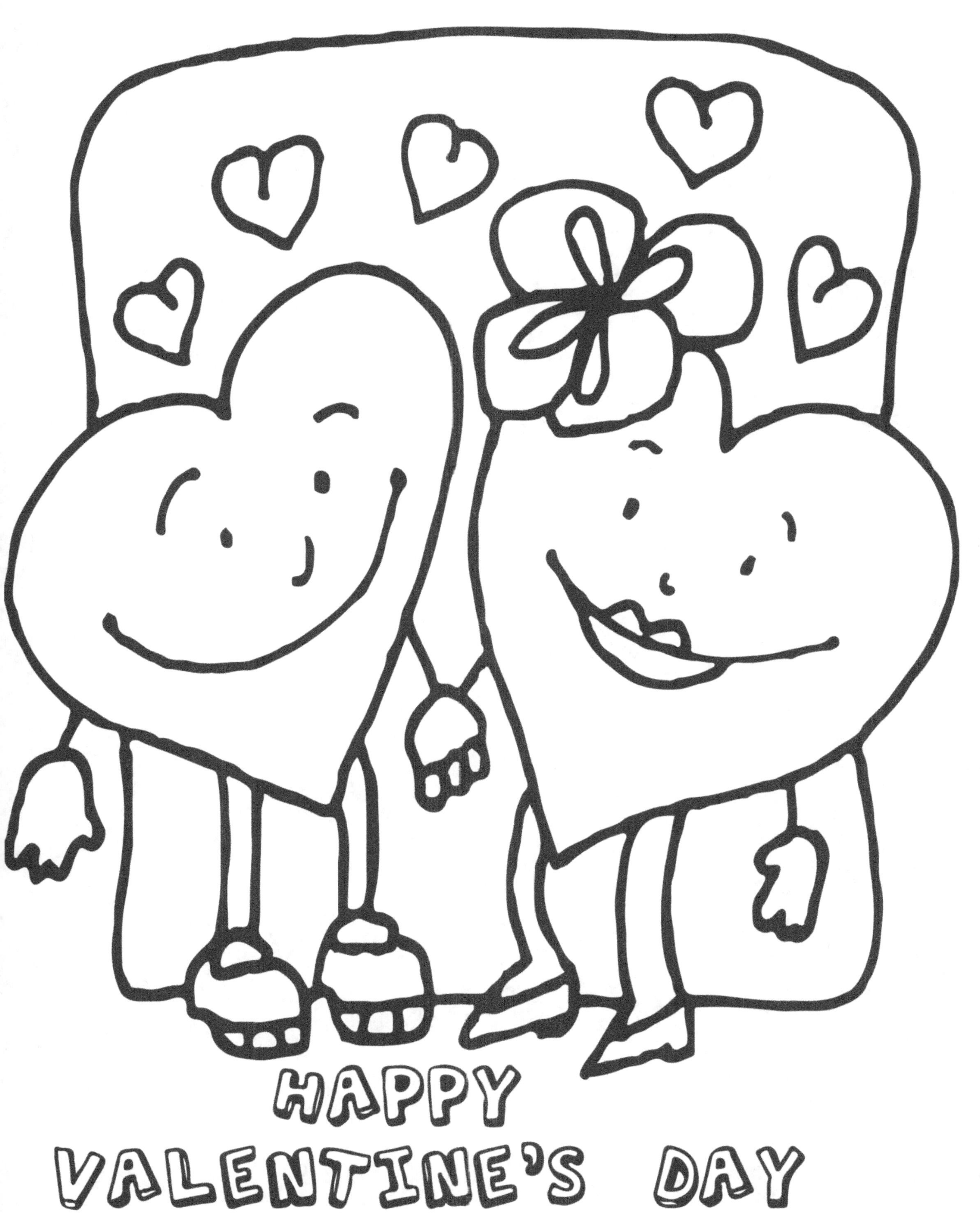

HAPPY
VALENTINE'S DAY

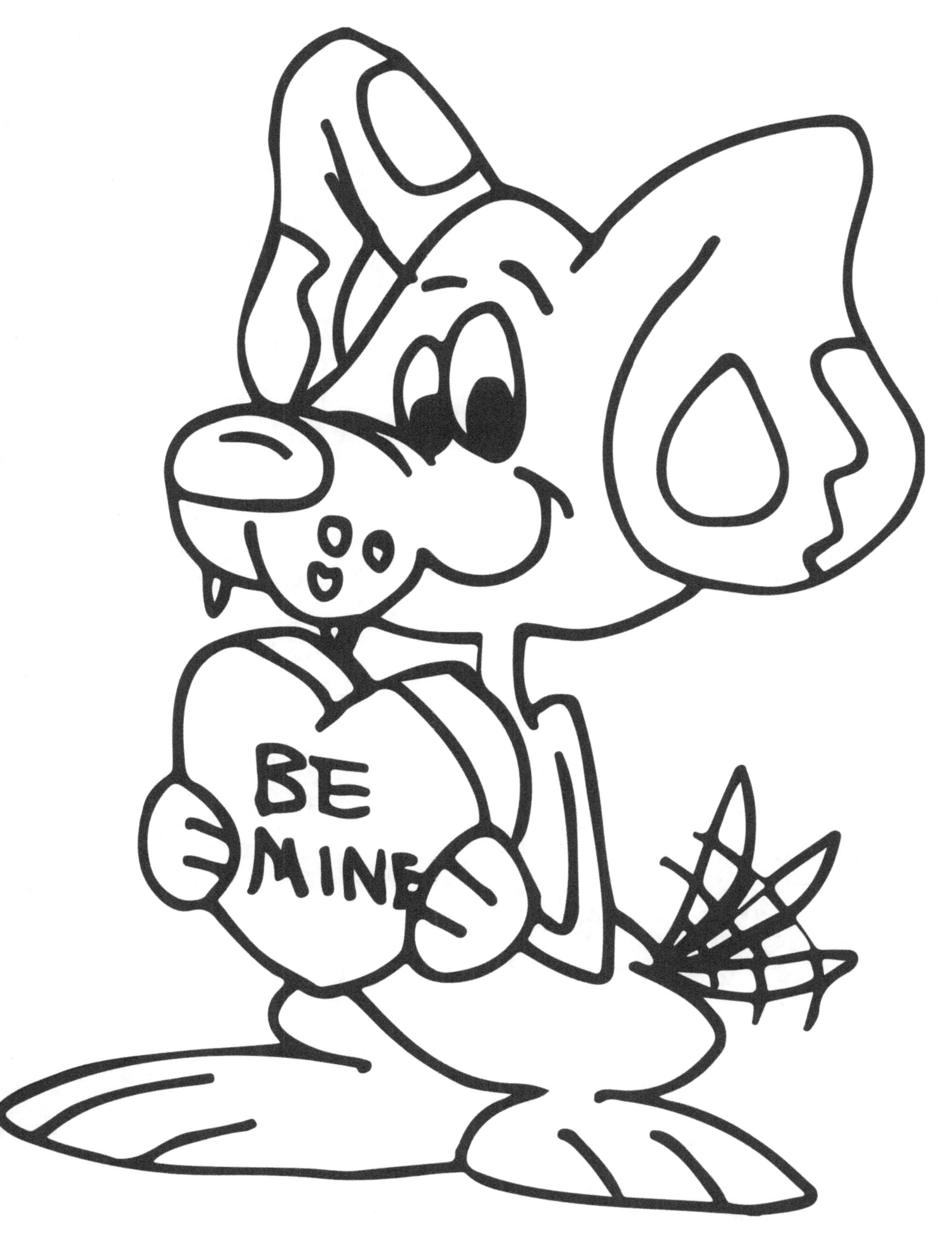
BE
MINE

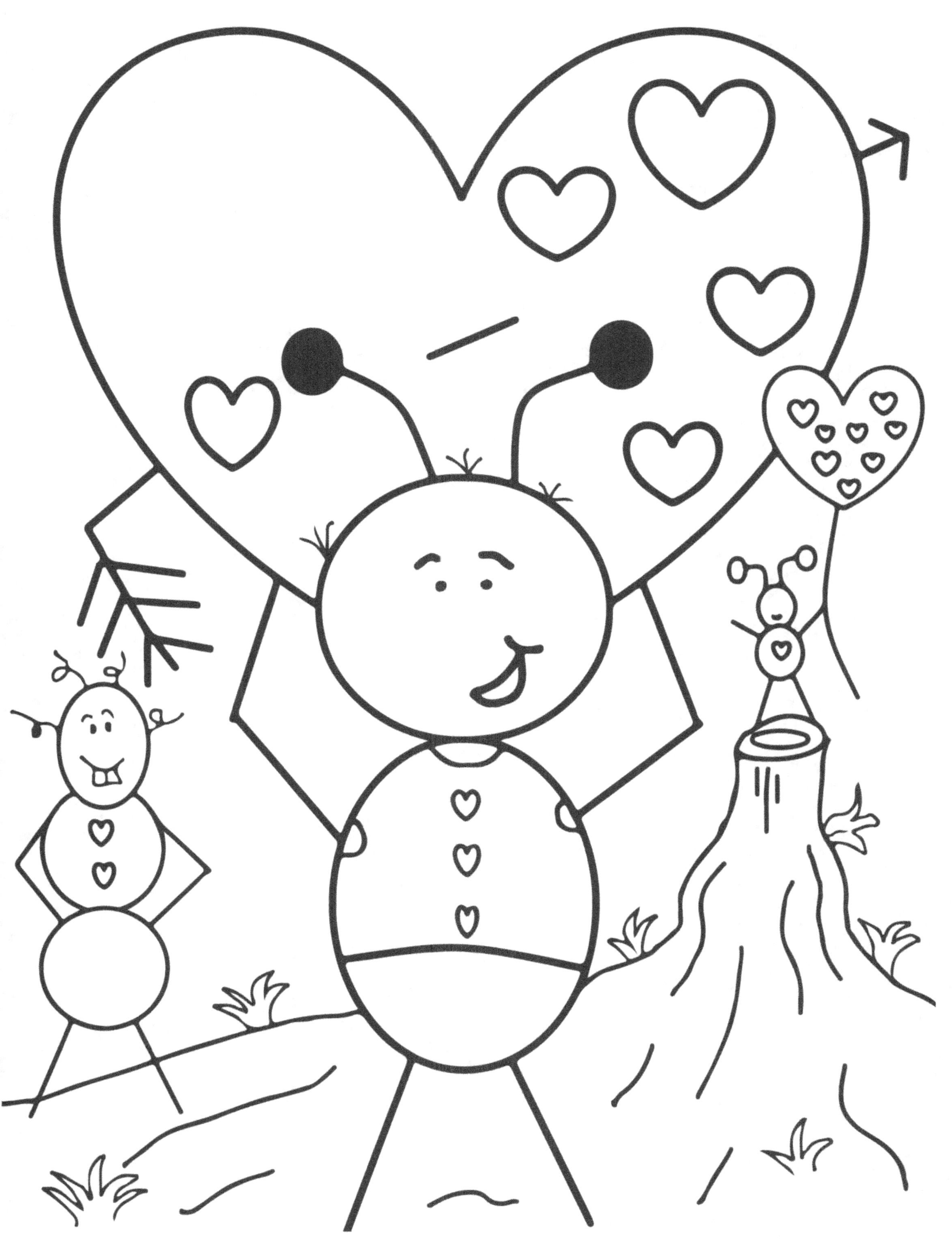

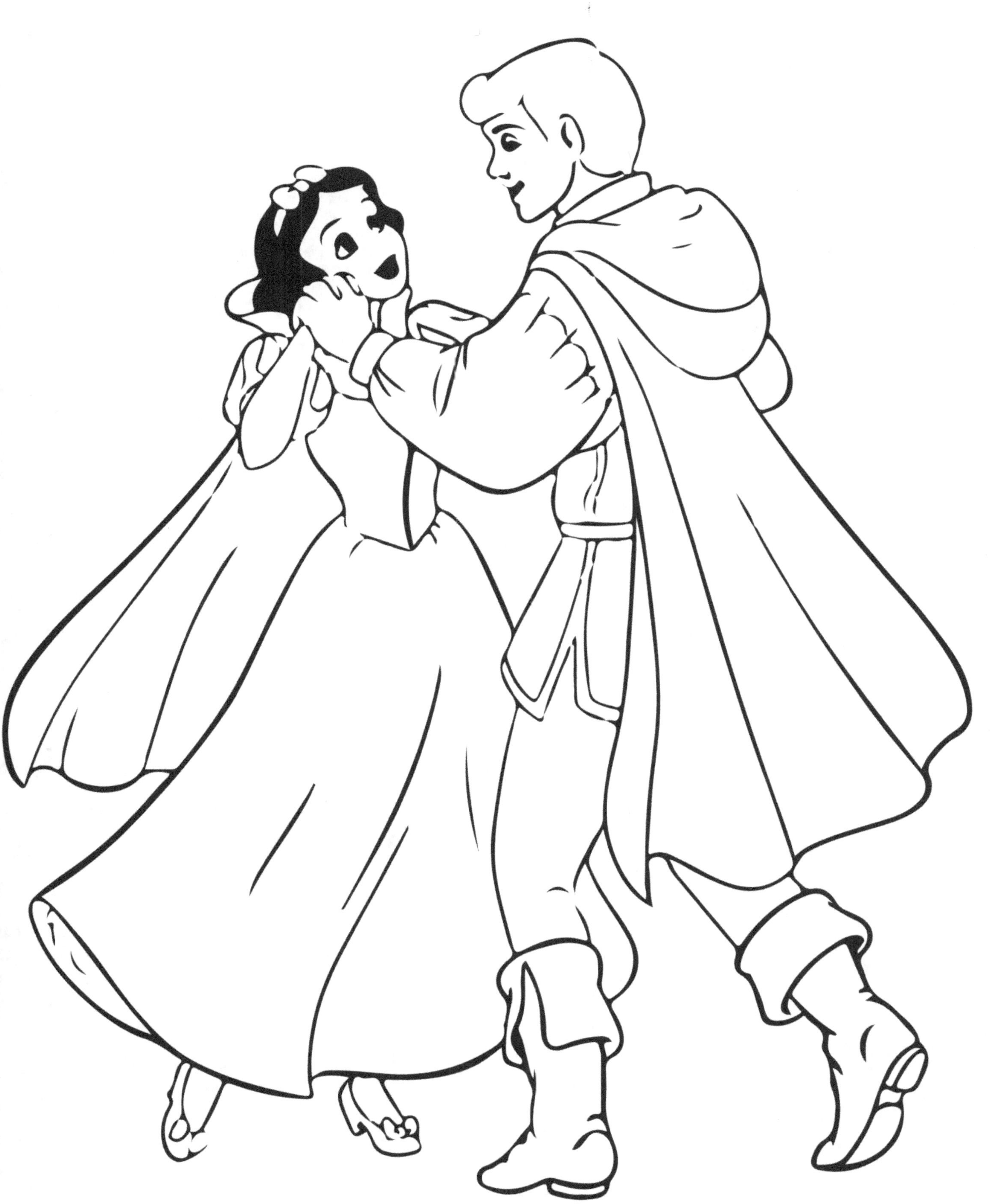

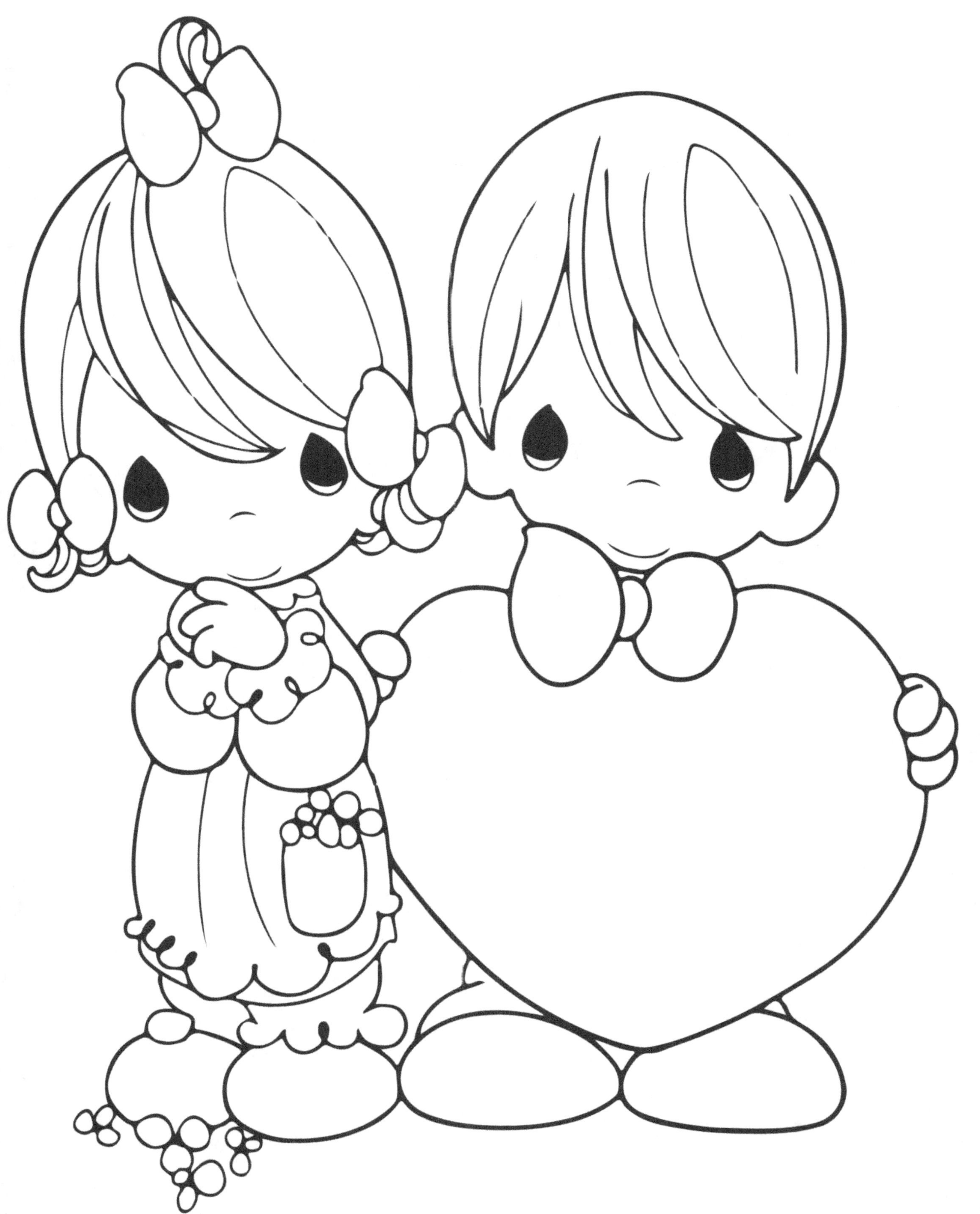

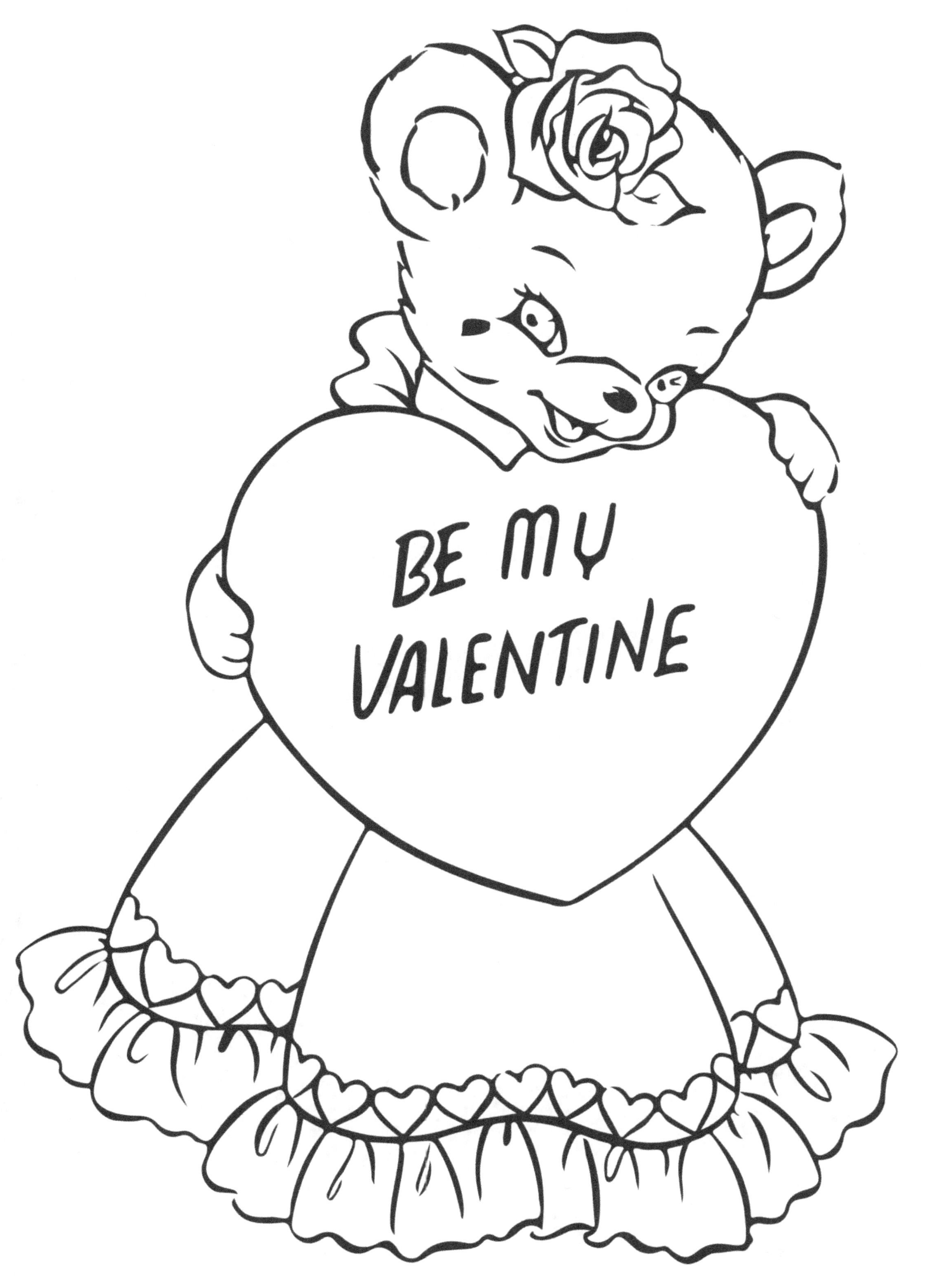

BE MY
VALENTINE

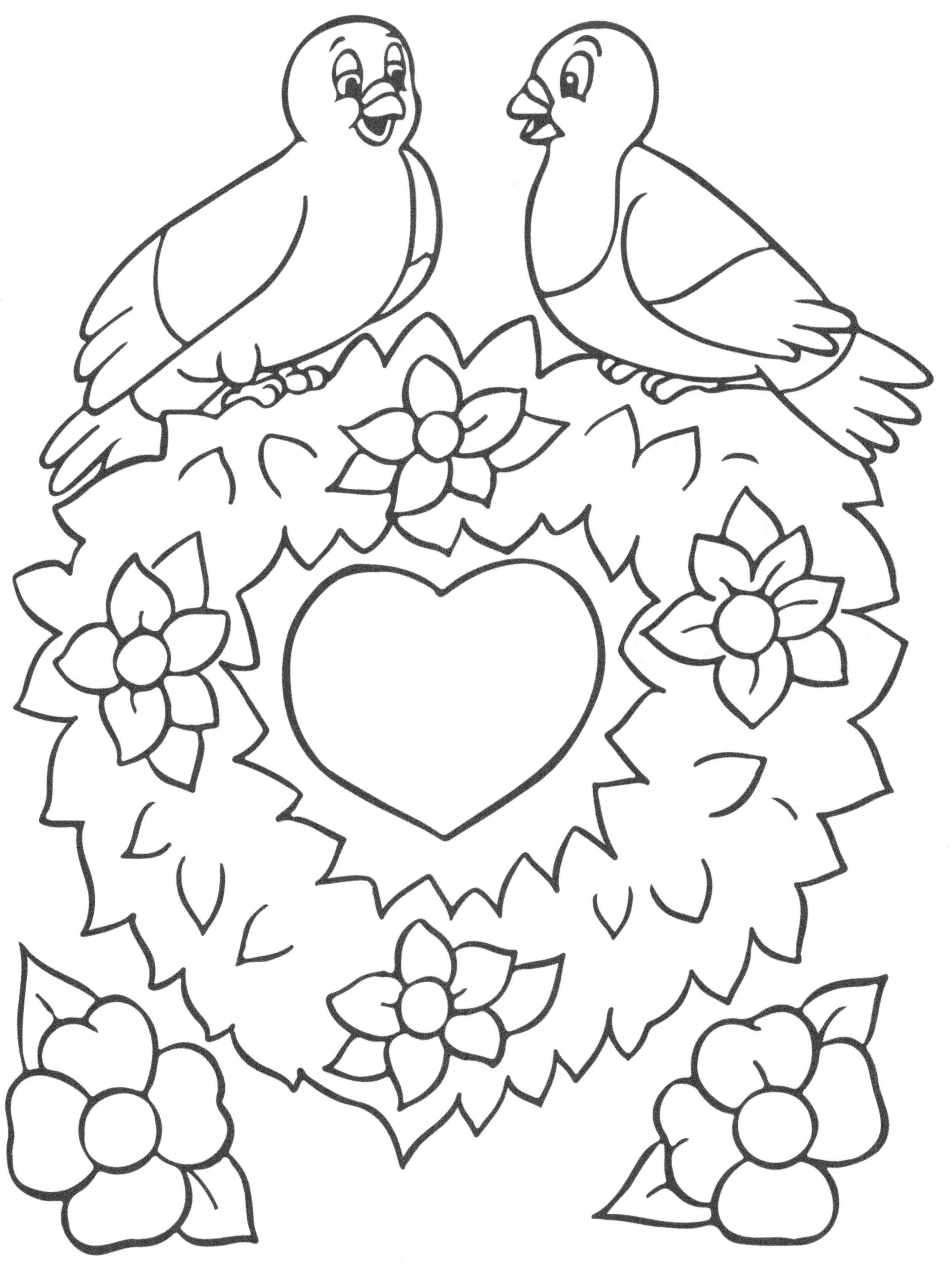

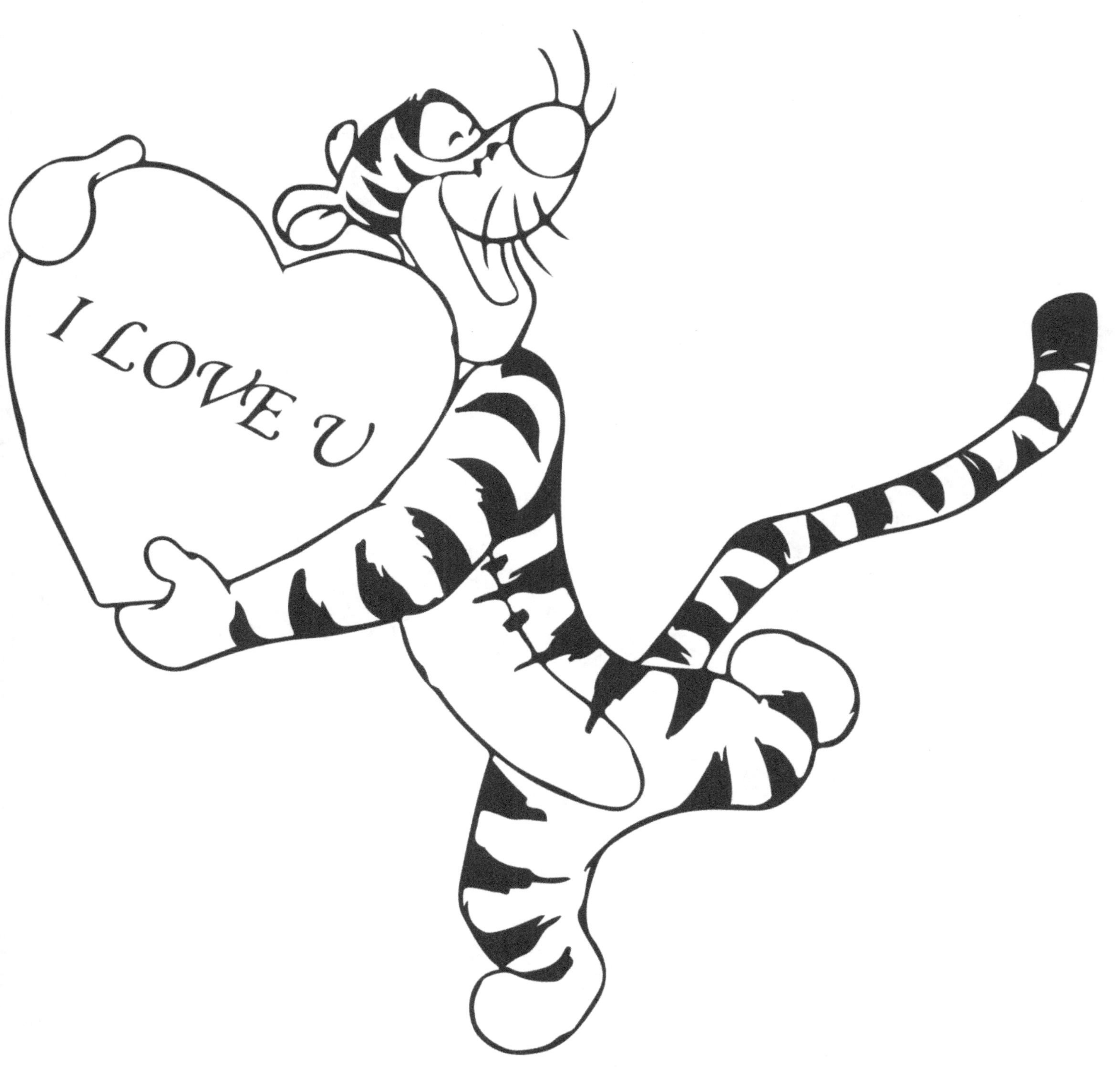
I LOVE U

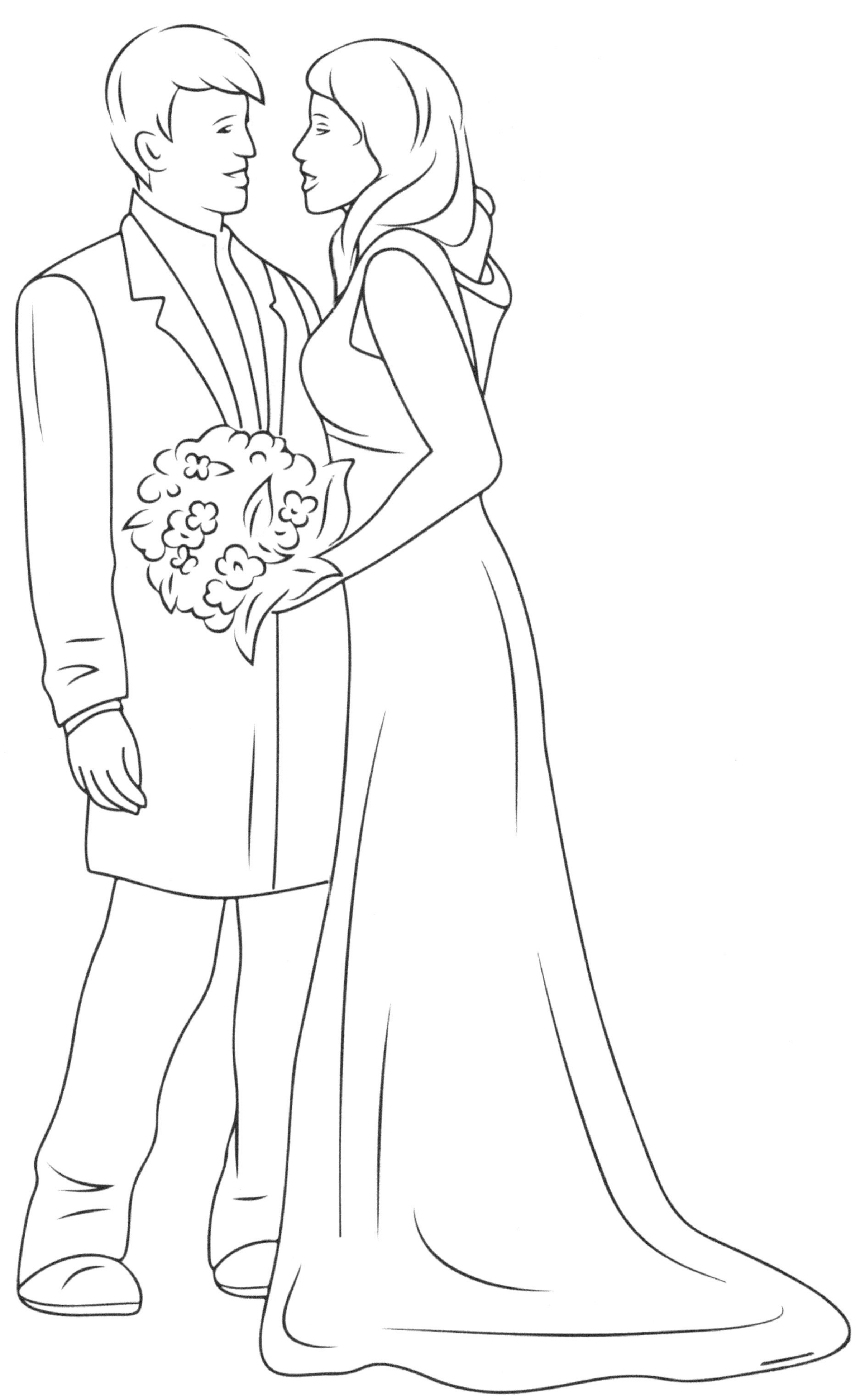

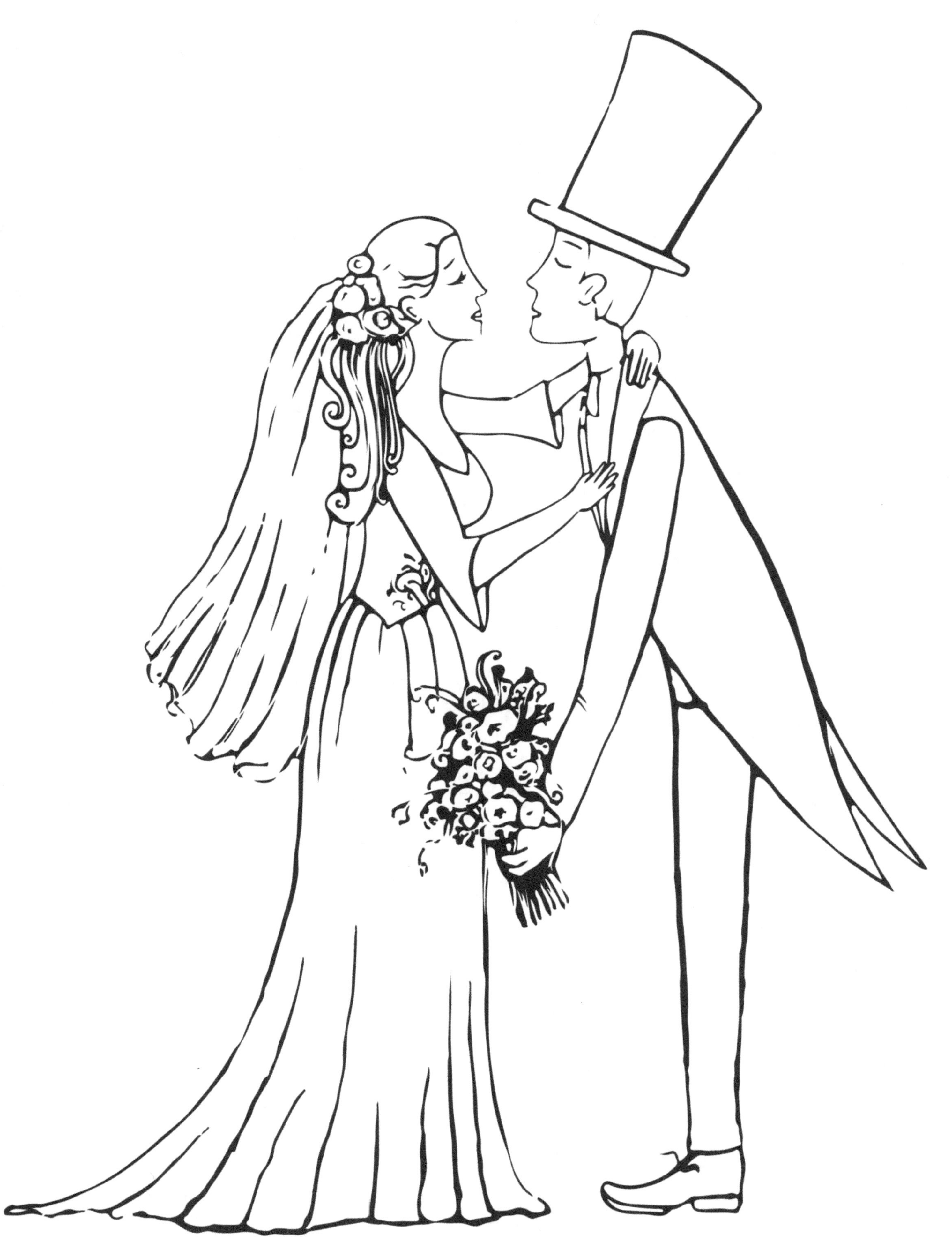

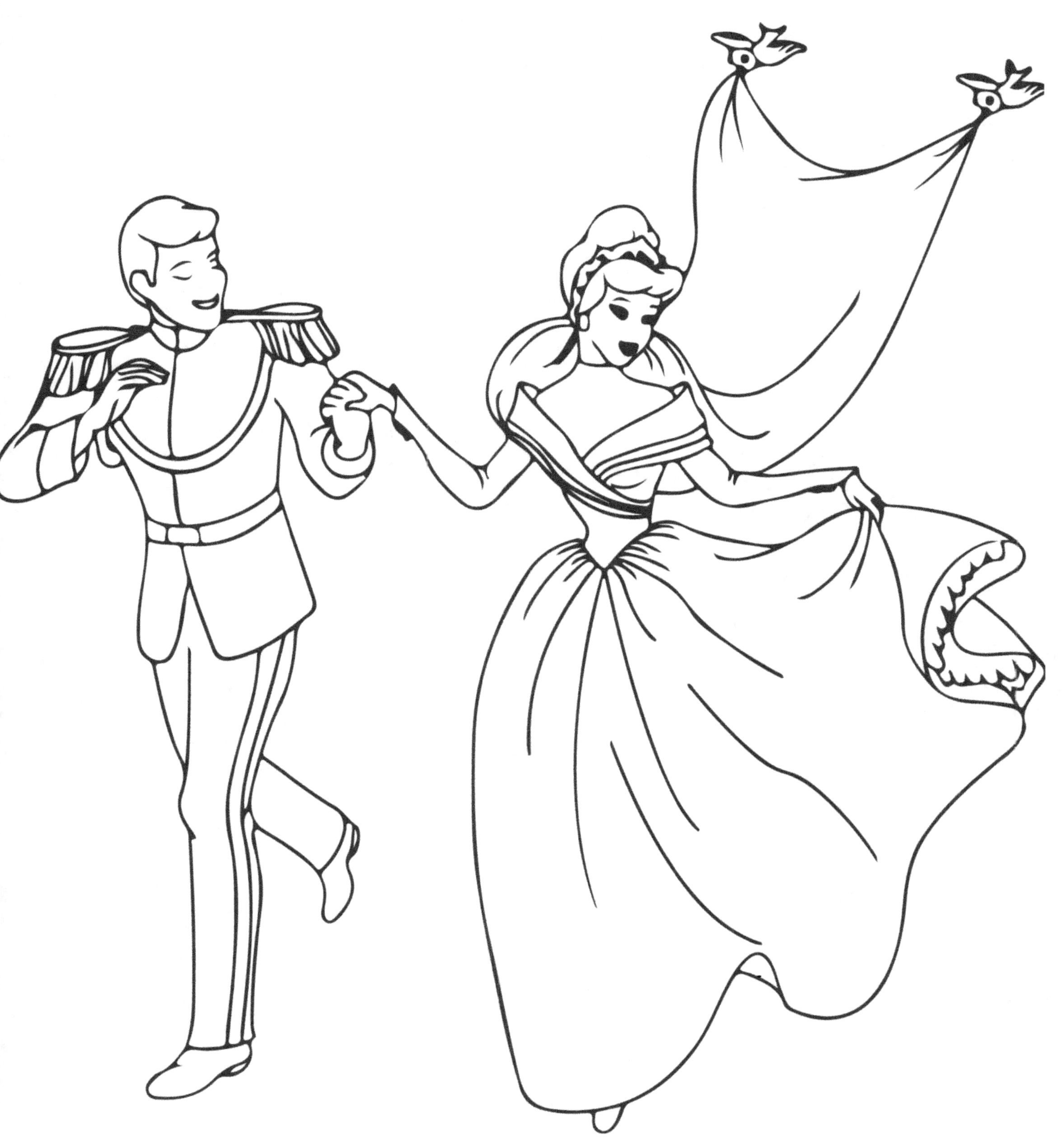

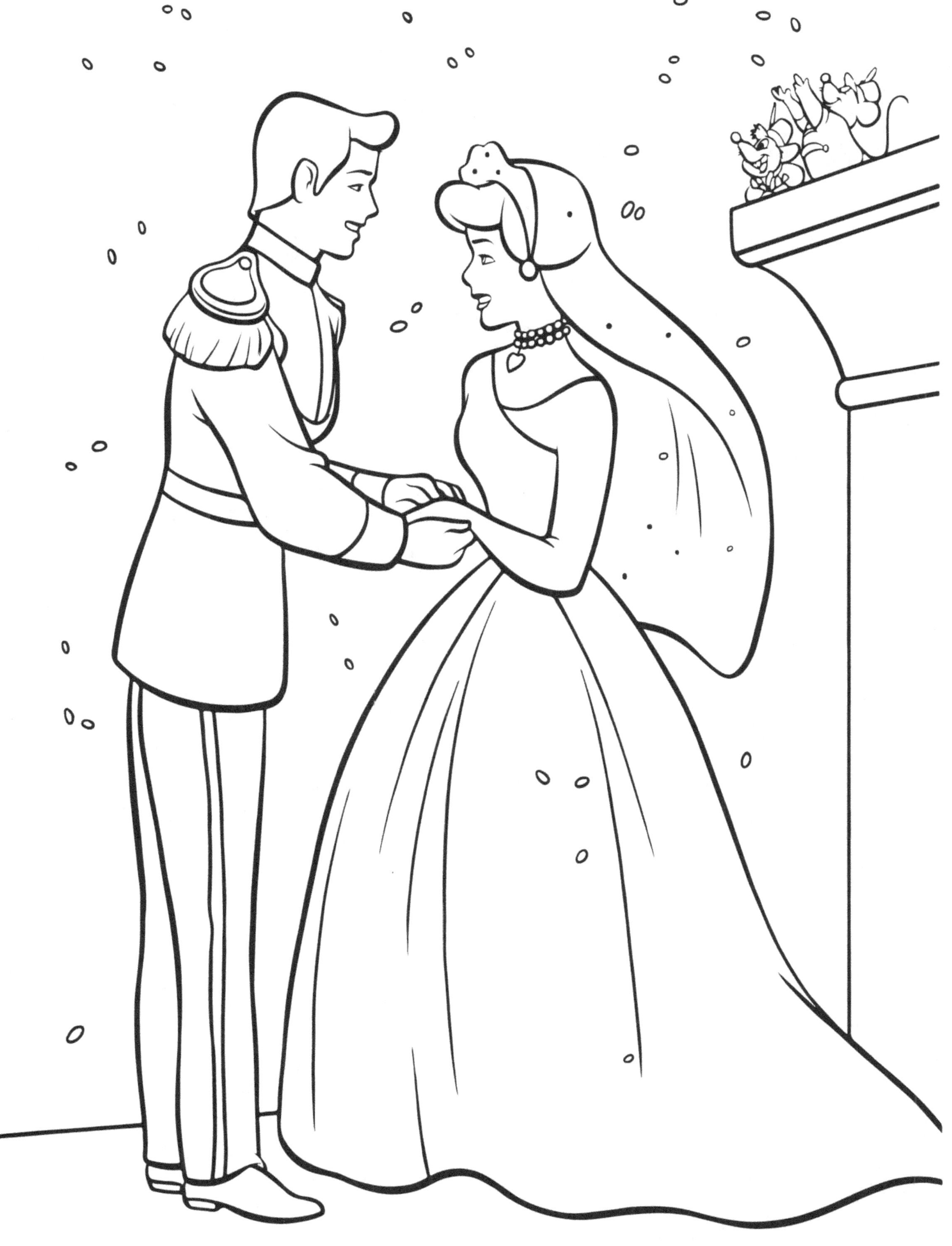

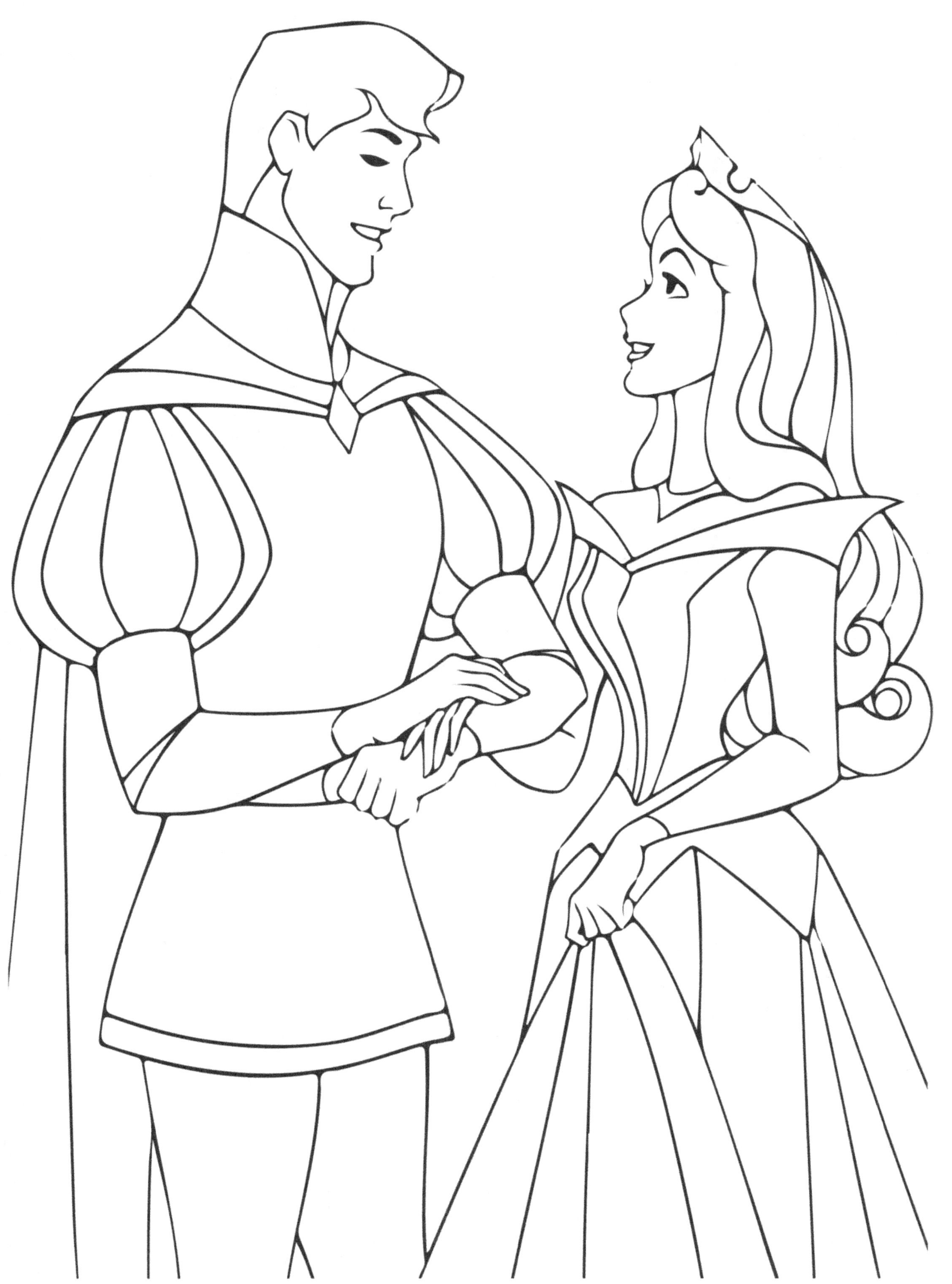

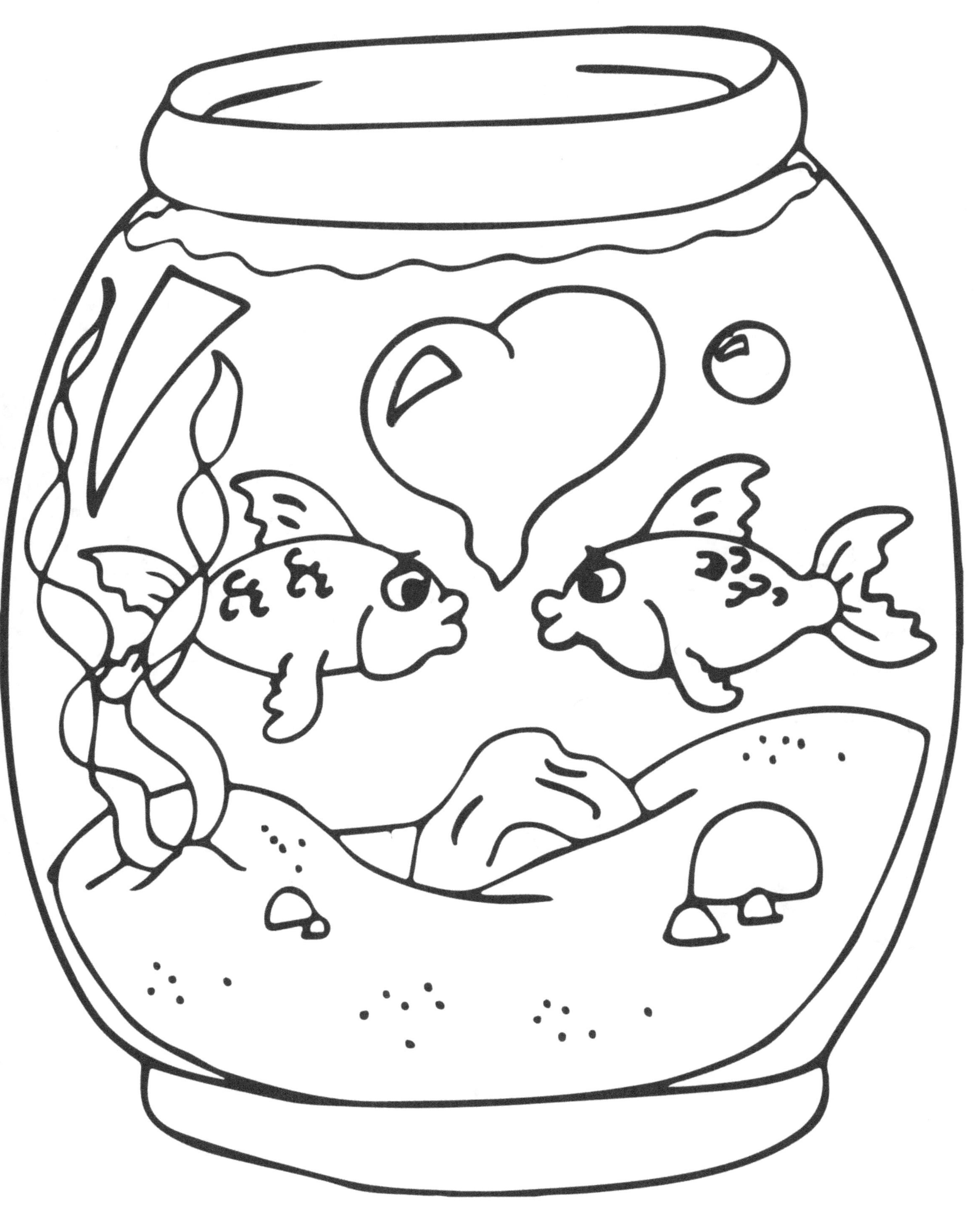

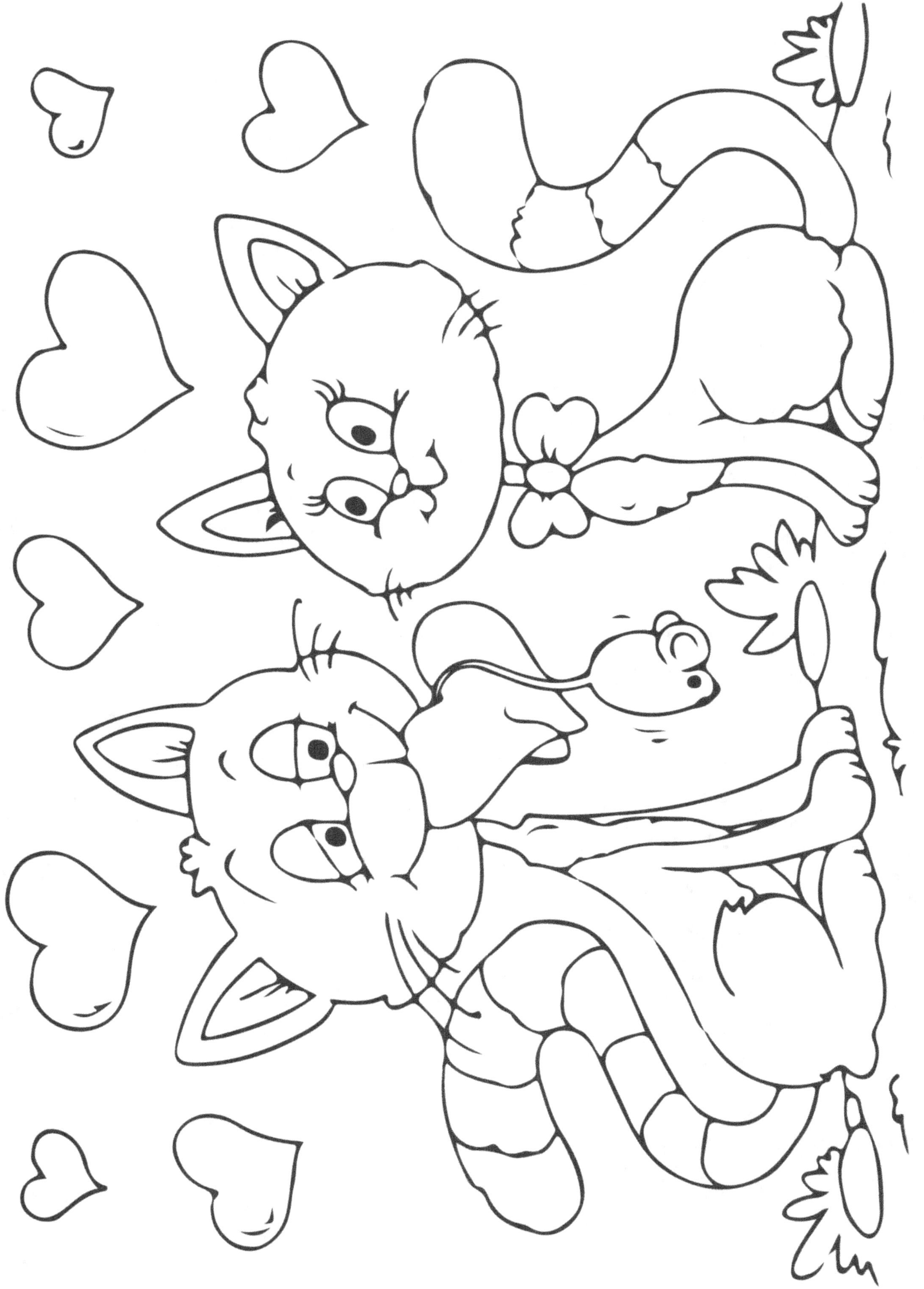

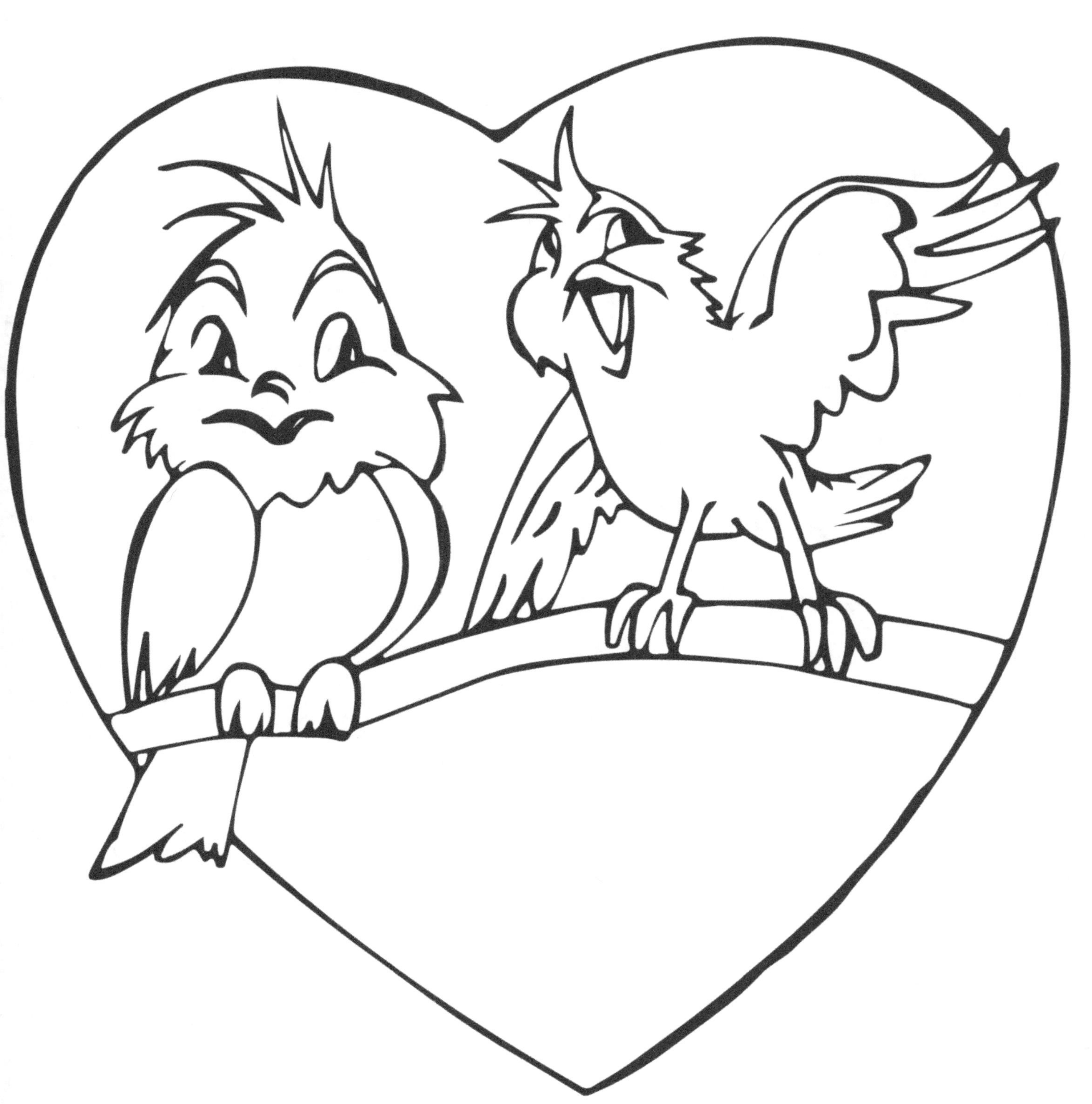

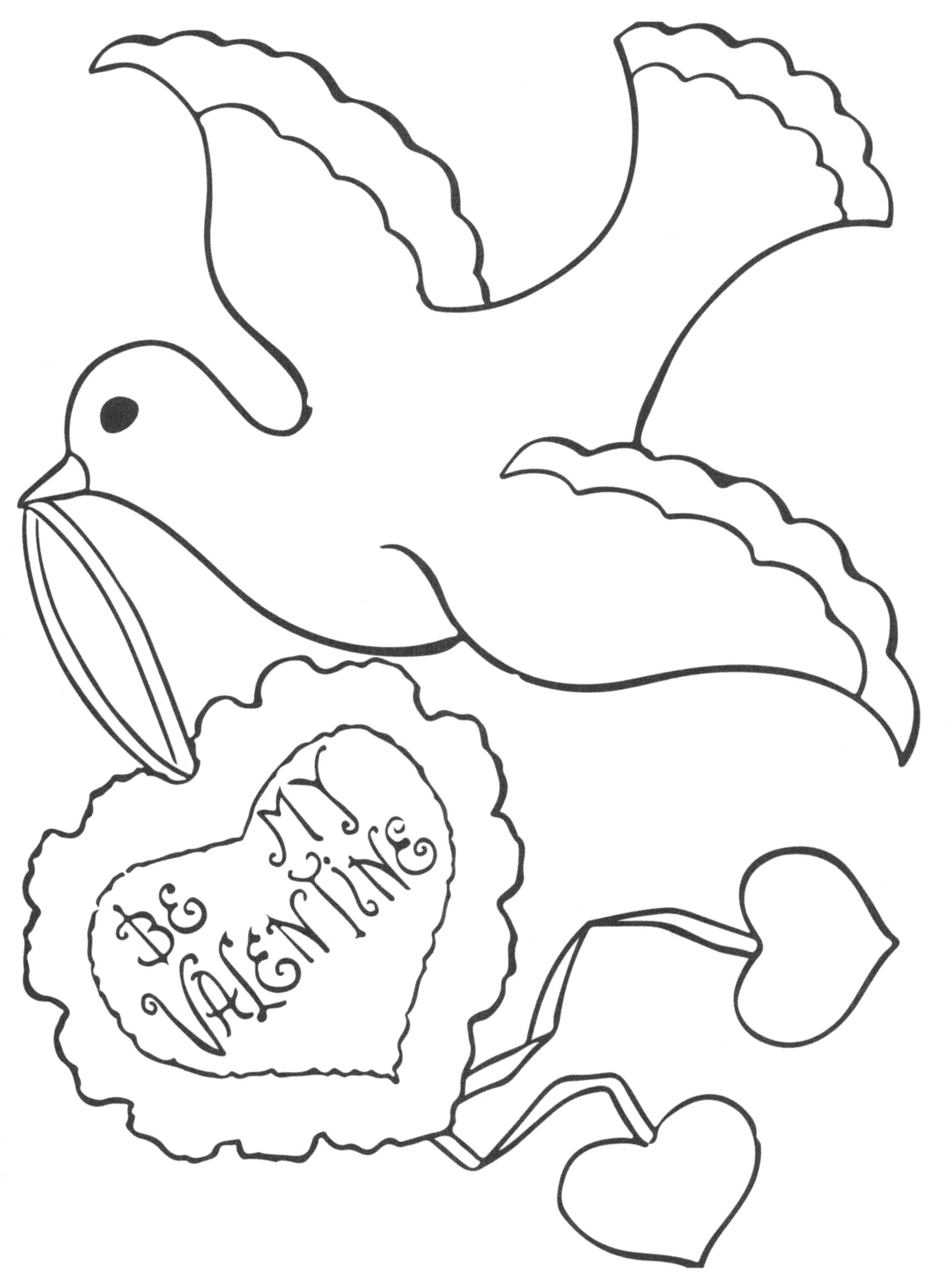

BE
MY
VALENTINE

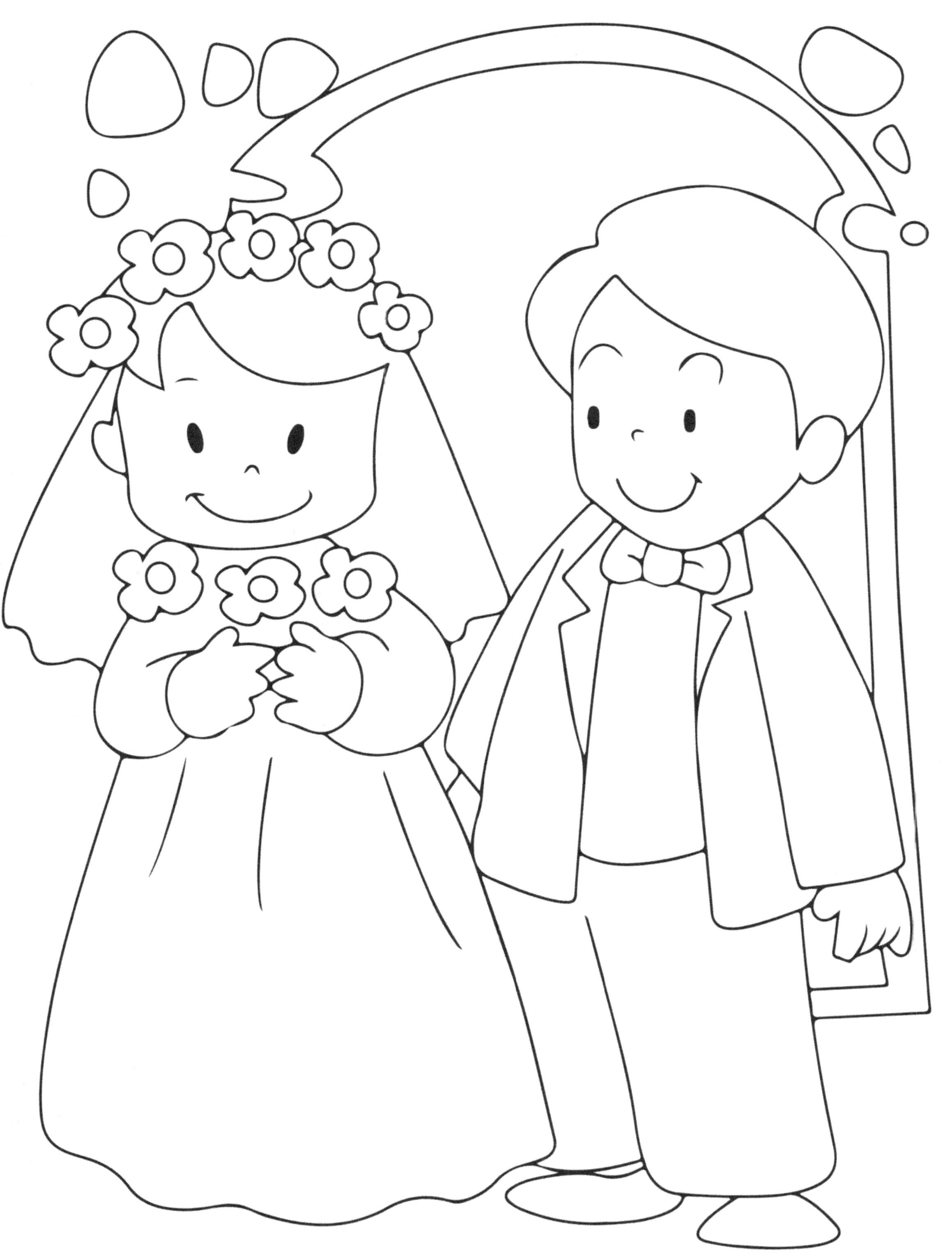

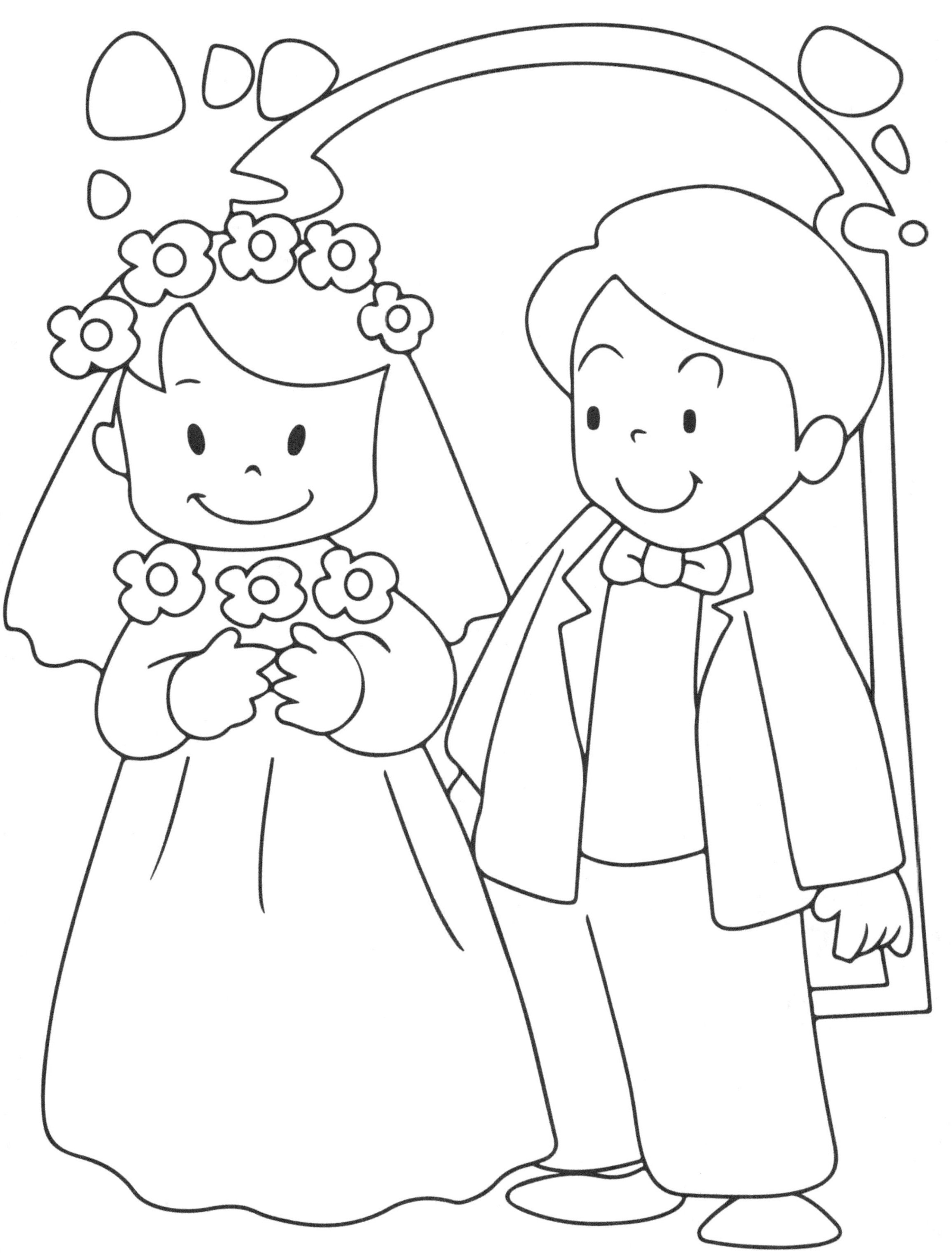

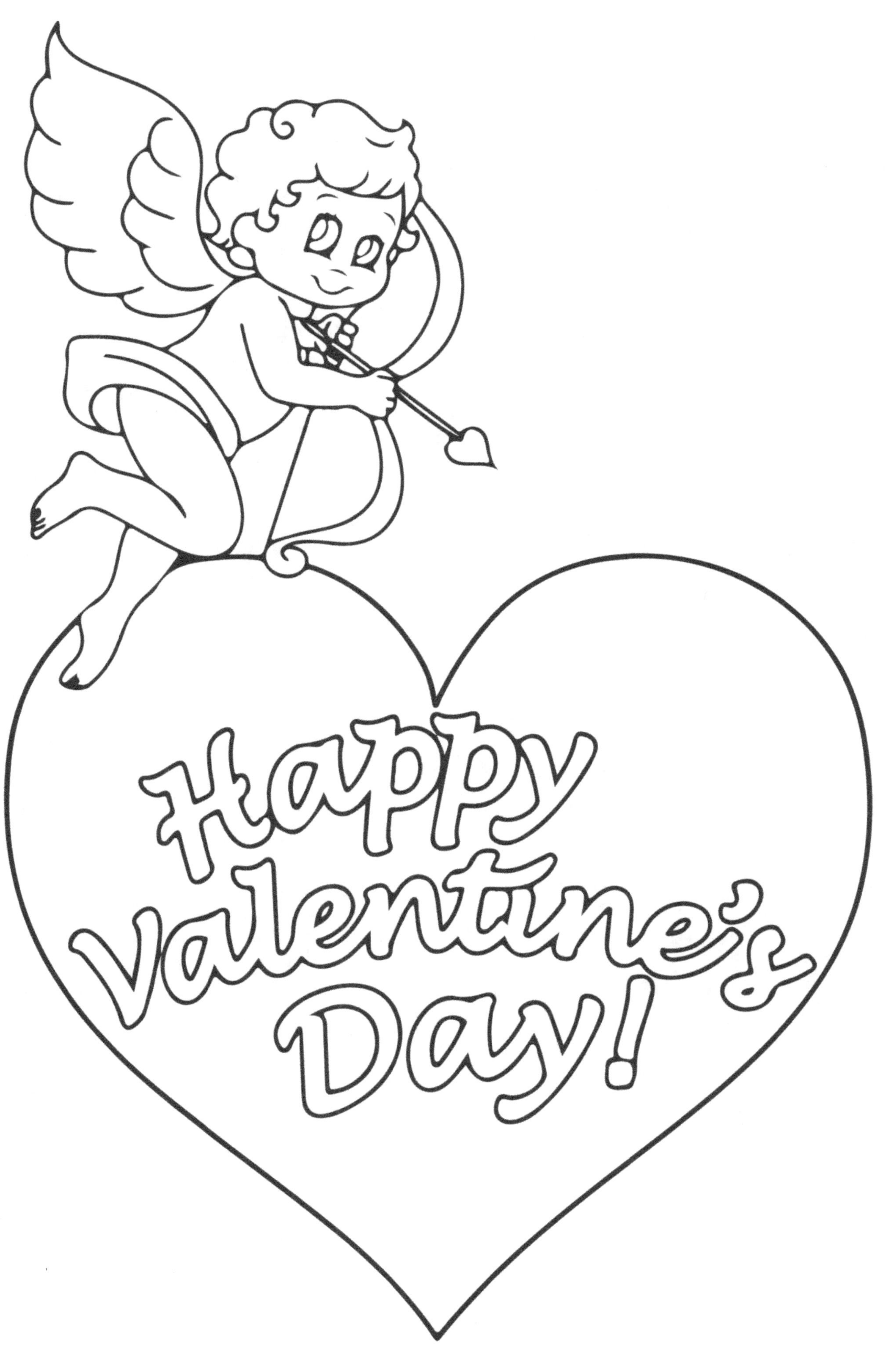

Happy Valentine's Day!

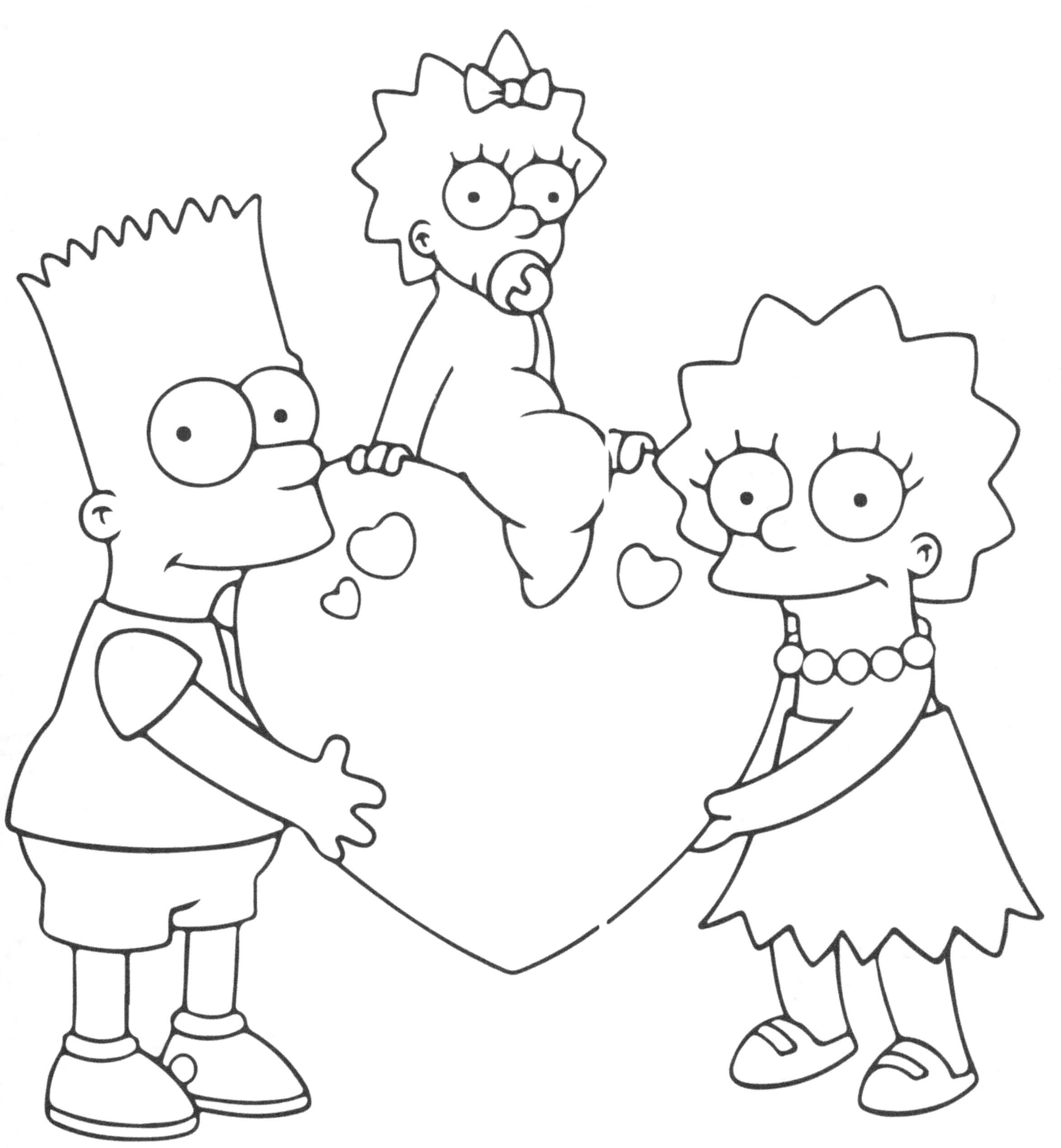

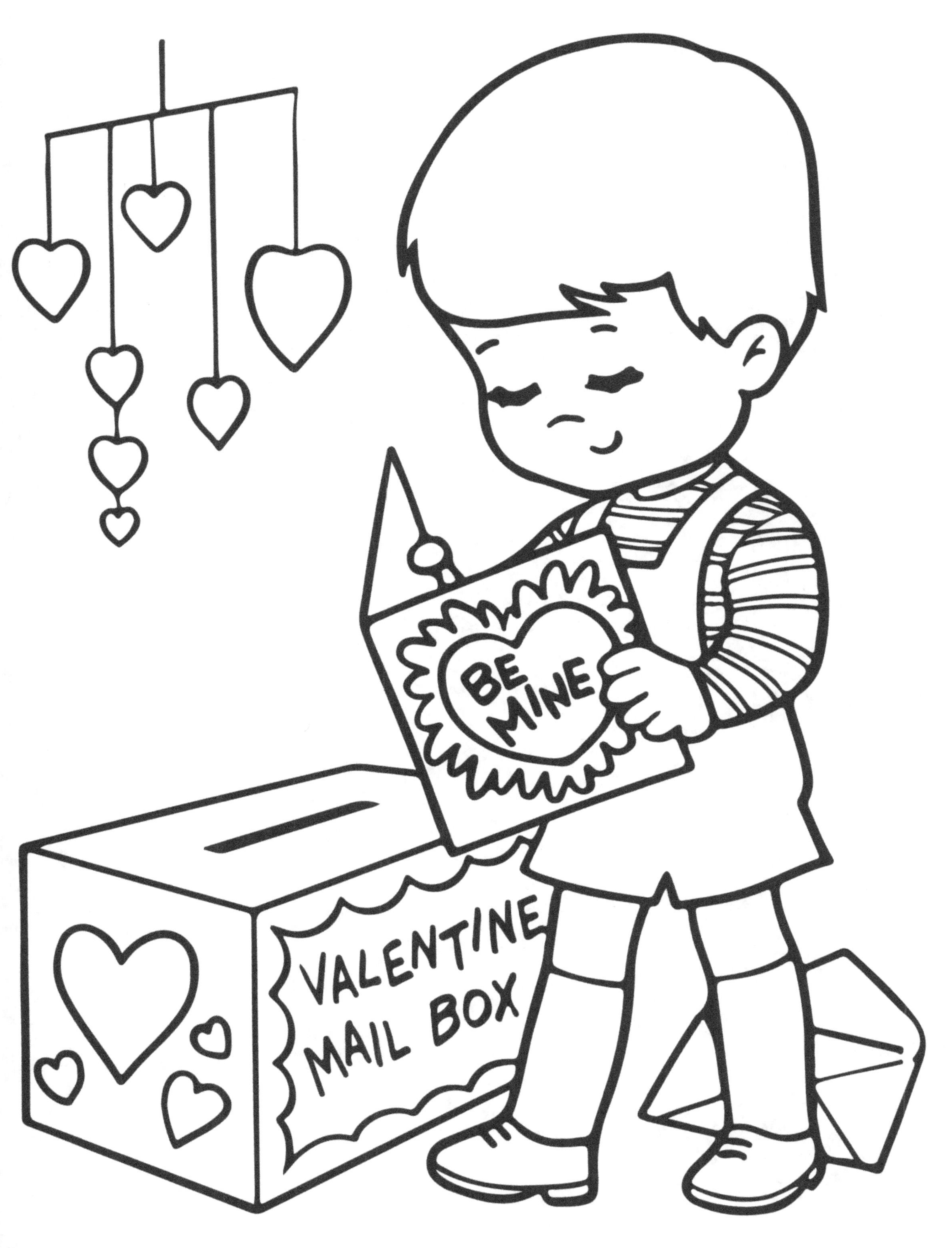

BE
MINE
VALENTINE
MAIL BOX